Toby and (and B...) and the Am... Jonah

by Peggy Hewitt

Illustrated by Tom Hewitt

Text copyright © Peggy Hewitt 1999
Illustrations copyright © Tom Hewitt 1999
The author asserts the moral right to be identified as the author of this work.
Published by
The Bible Reading Fellowship
Peter's Way, Sandy Lane West
Oxford OX4 5HG
ISBN 1 84101 055 3
First edition 1999
10 9 8 7 6 5 4 3 2 1 0
Acknowledgments
Unless otherwise stated, scripture quotations are taken from the Good News
Bible published by The Bible Societies/HarperCollins Publishers Ltd UK ©
American Bible Society, 1966, 1971, 1976, 1992.
A catalogue record for this book is available from the British Library.
Printed and bound in Great Britain by Caledonian Book Manufacturing
International, Glasgow.

Welcome to the Amazing Book of Jonah!

Jonah makes a break for it

Just imagine being swallowed by a large fish and spending three days in its 'innards'! Why Jonah?

In some ways, Jonah was like you and me. He really wanted to go God's way—until he decided his own way was best. God pointed in one direction—Jonah ran off in another.

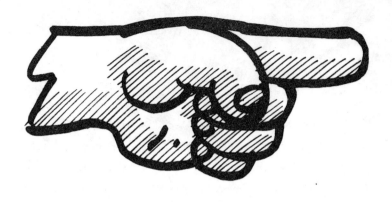

Jonah was a prophet, especially chosen by God to do his work. Yet here he is, managing to do everything wrong. He was stubborn, he had great adventures, and the way he got about was—well—amazing! Jesus knew about him and even compared himself to Jonah.

But before we read and enjoy his story, and learn more about God's love and patience, let's take a walk in Galilee...

Jesus and Jonah

The little town of Nazareth, where Jesus grew up, was less than an hour's walk away from Gath-hepher, where Jonah had lived and where his tomb was.

In the years before Jesus started teaching and healing people, he probably visited Jonah's tomb to sit in the shade and think about Jonah—about the sort of man he was and how much God had worked through him. Sometimes when you're sitting quietly

thinking about somebody, you feel you get to know them.

Jesus already knew and loved the story of Jonah and the big fish, which was written in the old scriptures of the Jewish people. Both Jesus and Jonah came from the district of Galilee.

So now, let's go back in time nearly three thousand years, to the start of Jonah's story...

Hearing God speak
Jonah 1:1

One day the Lord spoke to Jonah son of Amittai.

Because Jonah was a prophet, he spent a lot of time listening to God so that he could tell other people what he'd heard God say. (That's what being a prophet means.)

You may know somebody who is really nice, but they're a great chatterbox... chatter, chatter, chatter... and it's difficult for you to get a word in edgeways. This is especially annoying if you happen to be a chatterbox yourself!

We often talk about 'saying' our prayers. But praying is not just about 'saying'—it's also about listening. Sometimes we chatter away to God about our wants and our problems, and this is good. But we should also give God a chance to get a word in edgeways. We should be prepared to listen to what God has to say to us.

Try sitting quietly—anywhere. Think about how much God loves you—and listen to what he has to say.

This is a talking book

The low-down on Nineveh
Jonah 1:2

God said, 'Go to Nineveh, that great city, and speak out against it; I am aware how wicked its people are.'

If Jonah had been sitting on a stool as he listened to God saying this, he might just have fallen off it in surprise!

Nineveh was the capital of Assyria, the enemy of Israel. It was the last place in the world where Jonah would have thought of going to talk about God's love.

But God is full of surprises. He wanted Jonah to go there because, although Israel was very special to him, he was also God of all the world—even Nineveh.

Let us remember, at school or wherever we are, that Jesus is for everybody, whether they believe in him or not!

Going in the opposite direction
Jonah 1:3

Jonah, however, set out in the opposite direction in order to get away from the Lord. He went to Joppa, he found a ship about to go to Spain. He paid his fare and went aboard with the crew to sail to Spain, where he would be away from the Lord.

Sometimes, if we 'get out of bed on the wrong side' and are feeling cross, we do the opposite to what people want. Mum makes us toast for breakfast—so we have cornflakes instead. Or she says as we go out, 'Take your jacket,' but we don't—and probably get rained on.

Maybe Jonah had got out of bed on the wrong side. He was determined not to do what God wanted. God said, 'Go *east*—to Nineveh', but Jonah did the opposite. He booked a ticket on a ship sailing *west* from Joppa (today the town is called Jaffa) to faraway Spain.

There was a reason for Jonah behaving like this, which we will find out as we go along. A wrong reason! And could Jonah get away from God? Can we?

Go back nearly 300 pages...

A hop into Psalm 139
Psalm 139:7-12

Where could I go to escape from you? Where could I get away from your presence?
(Verse 7)

There was once a robber who stole thousands of pounds from a mail train. Then he escaped and went off to spend it all on the other side of the world. But he couldn't escape from himself and knowing what he'd done. When he was recaptured he felt glad.

There are lots of ways of running away. We can wear a wig or a false moustache and pretend we're somebody else. Or we can slam out of the room, run upstairs and lock our bedroom door. But sooner or later we've got to be ourselves, come downstairs, and face things.

It was the same for Jonah. However far he sailed, there was someone else on the boat who wasn't on the passenger list: God. Sooner or later Jonah would have to face him.

Things start going wrong
Jonah 1:4

But the Lord sent a strong wind on the sea, and the storm was so violent that the ship was in danger of breaking up.

Have you ever been on a small ship in rough seas? I have—and I'll never forget it. The wind seems to be in complete control. When the ship sails into the waves the front rears up and then crashes down with a roar. It's even worse when the waves hit the ship's side... it rolls as if it's going to turn right over. You can't stand up and everything is hurtling about. Just imagine you're on a small ship—in a storm.

But we know as we read this Amazing Book that God is in control. He sent that wind for a reason!

Sometimes when we hit a rough patch we forget that God is in control—if we'll let him be.

Heavenly Father, help us to trust you, especially when we're going through a stormy time.

Whoops! I think a leg's come off the sofa

10

Jonah 1:1-4

Things to do

Way out SPAIN

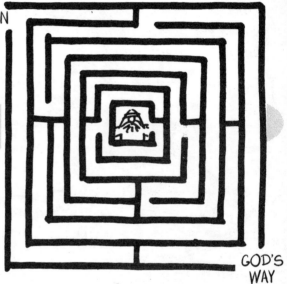

There are lots of ways that Jonah can go. Or are there? See if you can find a way out for him.

GOD'S WAY

Toby + Trish | Way out

Why are you walking into the kitchen backwards, Trish?

I'm half an hour late, so it looks as though I'm just going out

SPAIN

MEDITERRANEAN SEA

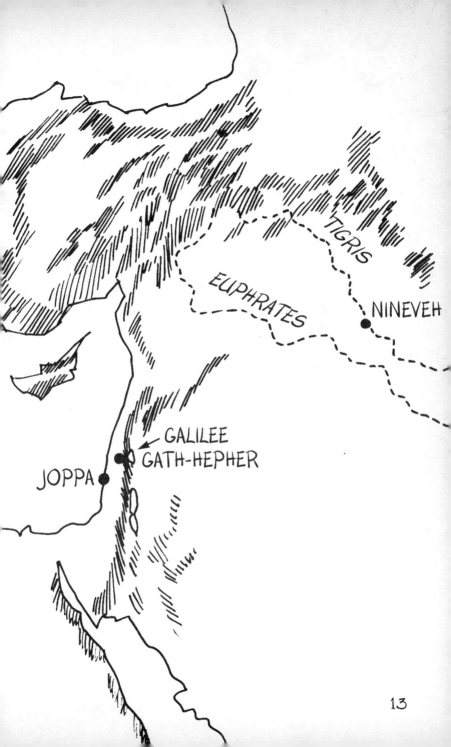

TIGRIS

EUPHRATES

NINEVEH

GALILEE
GATH-HEPHER

JOPPA

What do we do?
Jonah 1:5a

The sailors were terrified and cried out for help, each one to his own god.

It must have been a terrible storm to throw those sailors into such a state. Storms in the Mediterranean Sea often blow up very quickly (that's where I had *my* storm experience) and the sailors were used to them. But this one was different.

Just imagine tough sailors crying out for help. But to whom? Their prayers were flying in different directions—like the wind-tossed seabirds—and reaching... nobody.

The 'Joppa-to-Spain ferry' had no lifeboat. If it sank, that would be the end of them. God had no plan to sink the boat—but everybody needed shaking up a bit in order to get real.

It's so much better if we get to know God and his love now, *before* we find ourselves in a '999' situation.

Imagine carrying the shopping for ever

Throw it overboard
Jonah 1:5b

Then, in order to lessen the danger, they threw the cargo overboard.

If you were aiming to win an Olympic gold medal (you never know—you might some day!), you'd have to be careful not to put on too much weight. It would slow you down and you'd soon get tired. Just imagine walking about with five bags of sugar strapped to you—five kilos of extra weight. Phew! That would make you huff and puff.

Jonah's ship was in trouble. The only thing to do was to lessen the weight so that it would ride higher in the water and sail better. Less baggage on board—an easier trip.

We sometimes carry too much 'baggage' around. Things we possess, things we worry about. We can feel weighed down by problems.

God wants us to travel light. You'll have much more fun if you keep it simple.

Jonah past caring
Jonah 1:5c

Meanwhile, Jonah had gone below and was lying in the ship's hold, sound asleep.

Whatever you're so gloomy about, it's not worth it!

Winnie the Pooh had a friend called Eeyore who was very, very GLOOMY. Eeyore, as you can guess, was a donkey. His voice was gloomy, his thoughts were gloomy, he even lived at the Gloomy Place. When things went wrong for Eeyore he just gave up, stayed by himself, and thought how bad things were.

Jonah must have been feeling like that. Things were going badly wrong—he was past caring. He didn't think to help the sailors. He took himself off, in spite of the storm, and he slept.

Sometimes when things go wrong we shut ourselves off—even from those who love us best. We feel gloomy about how bad things are—for us.

Our Father, help us always to be open to your love and to accept your help.

Don't just lie there
Jonah 1:6a

*The captain found him there and said to him,
'What are you doing asleep?'*

Whatever was it that made the ship's captain leave the sailors on deck, desperately trying to keep the ship afloat? Some people think that Jonah was snoring so loudly that the captain came to investigate. They must have been very loud snores!

Or maybe he'd noticed something different about Jonah and had him on his mind. How could a man sleep through that storm? But being different was no excuse for shirking. The captain needed 'all hands on deck'.

Sometimes we feel we've got a lot on our minds and we don't notice what's going on around us. But even on the cross Jesus could think about his mother, his friends, and the men dying with him.

*Heavenly Father, help us not to be so
involved with how we're feeling that we
forget other people.*

Oh, thanks, Toby. I've just trodden on your best CD!

17

What would people ask us to do?
Jonah 1:6b

'Get up and pray to your god for help.'

'For goodness' sake, do something!' The captain hadn't met anybody like Jonah before. Here was a man whose god seemed very real to him—and very important. It was obvious that Jonah was wrestling with a great problem. Jonah might not have been his usual self, but God was still such a part of his life that it showed through even this.

Somehow the frantic captain could see that Jonah believed in a god who actually cared what happened to him in his everyday life. Then why the storm?

We also believe in this true God when we become friends of Jesus. It would be wonderful to think that people could see Jesus in our everyday lives—and who knows what could happen then!

When Boomerang is hungry, he looks just like Toby!

Jonah 1:5–6
Things to do
Filming a storm

When you see a programme on television where people are supposed to be in a cabin on a boat which is rolling from side to side, very often it's the *camera* which is rolling from side to side while the actors just bump into each other to give the right effect.

Make a television screen out of a cereal carton and tilt it, and your head, from side to side. If you have a friend or two to run to the left when you tilt to the right, it's even better! Change places and let them see the effect.

Toby + Trish — Ups and downs

I wonder why it's called a see-saw?

It should be called a sea-sick

11

The captain tries plan 'C'
Jonah 1:6c

'Maybe your god will feel sorry for us and spare our lives.'

There's a saying that started amongst sailors—'Any port in a storm'—meaning that if you can't get to where you were going originally, anywhere is better than the ship sinking. In other words, if plan 'A' fails, turn to plan 'B', then even plan 'C'. Now everybody uses the saying. We'll try anything if we're desperate.

The captain was desperate. Plan 'A'—sailing to Spain—had failed. So had plan 'B'—praying to their own gods. Now he was willing to try plan 'C'. After all, it wasn't *his* fault that Jonah had chosen to sail on his ship. And maybe this God who could whip up a storm at will could also save them. Maybe.

But our God is not a God of 'maybe'. He is the God of 'definitely'. He loves, and will save, everybody—even those whose faith is just beginning. Read on!

Plan ZZZZZZZZ

The only thing I ever won was a beautiful baby contest

Who's to blame?
Jonah 1:7

The sailors said to one another, 'Let us draw lots and find out who is to blame for getting us into this danger.' They did so, and Jonah's name was drawn.

Sometimes, if we're feeling guilty about something, we try to hide it. But sooner or later it gets out. So it's best to come clean to start with.

Jonah was not feeling comfortable with himself. How could he be—running away from God? Hiding in the hold of the ship was no use.

And the winner of the sailors' lottery was—surprise, surprise—Jonah! At last he was brought face to face with what he had done. God, who was still in complete control of Jonah, used even the sailors' lottery in his plan.

Sometimes we think that God is only interested in 'church' and 'religious' things. Not so. He is interested in—and can work in—every single part of our lives.

O o r u?

Jonah 1:8

So they said to Jonah, 'Now then, tell us! Are you to blame for this? What are you doing here? What country do you come from? What is your nationality?'

There's a strange caterpillar in *Alice in Wonderland* who wears Turkish slippers on his many feet and a Turkish hat on his head. He sits on a leaf and smokes a Turkish hookah pipe with a long tube that blows bubbles in a bowl of water. Yuk! When he blows smoke out of his mouth it forms the question, 'Oo r u?'

The sailors naturally wanted to know who Jonah was, and what he was up to. He had to be certain about this himself.

Who are *we?* There's a song that gives us the answer:

For you gave me a heart and you gave me
a smile,
You gave me Jesus and you made me your child,
And I just thank you, Father, for making me ME.

We are ourselves, and we are very special to God.

The Lord of sea and sky
Jonah 1:9

'I am a Hebrew,' Jonah answered. 'I worship the Lord, the God of heaven, who made land and sea.'

Jonah didn't exactly answer their questions. But what he did say was the most important thing in his life. 'I worship the Lord.' Ten out of ten for Jonah here. Battered by the waves on the outside, miserable on the inside, faced by a crew of angry sailors, he could still say that. Why?

Because he realized that his Lord was in charge of everything that ever was, and is, and will be. The furthest star, the smallest flower, the newest baby, belong to him.

The wonder is that Jonah's Lord is our Lord, too. We can know his love, his patience and his greatness by allowing Jesus to guide us.

Mighty Father, help us to know that you made the world and everything in it—then to show this in our lives.

Confession time!
Jonah 1:10a

Jonah went on to tell them that he was running away from the Lord.

Having said all that about his Lord, Jonah must have felt pretty silly admitting he was running away from him. But he's come clean at last—his guilty secret is out. He's had the courage to admit it—maybe he's not so bad after all. At least the sailors would know him now, and understand him.

It's not always easy to own up when we've done something silly or wrong. But if we've got the courage to say we're sorry first to God, then to anybody we might have hurt, it will help us get 'back on the rails' again. Sometimes there's something we can do to prove we're sorry.

Saying 'sorry' is like taking a heavy weight off your back. And Jesus took that weight away from us, on to himself, when he died on the cross.

It was me but it was the wind as well

Jonah 1:6-10
Things to do
Hands up who's got it

You'll need a long length of string and a ring—you could use a Polo mint. Put the ring on the string and knot the ends of the string together. Get as many friends as you can to stand in a circle holding the string tightly with both hands. Ask one person to stand in the middle.

Everybody holding the string slides their hands backwards and forwards as if they are passing the ring, and the ring is quickly passed round the circle. The person in the centre has to guess who is holding the ring by tapping a hand. When they guess correctly, whoever had the ring changes places with the guesser and goes into the middle.

Toby + Trish   Hands down

It was me, Sir!

You were the worst of the junior readers, Toby?

Sorry, Sir! I thought you said who was the first in the hundred metres

25

Realizing the truth
Jonah 1:10b

The sailors were terrified and said to him, 'That was an awful thing to do!'

There's a story about a little boy called Pinocchio. His father, Geppetto, made him out of wood, but Geppetto loved him so much that Pinocchio was given real life. Like all little boys (and girls), he sometimes did what he shouldn't and Jiminy Cricket, splendid with top hat and large umbrella, tried to stop him. Not always successfully! Jiminy was Pinocchio's conscience—that little voice that sometimes says, 'Just a minute—this is awful!'

We all have a conscience—a little, unexpected voice inside us that speaks up and makes us realize we're doing what we shouldn't.

The sailors were like Jonah's conscience. They were from another country and worshipped other gods, but, unexpectedly, they spoke the truth and made Jonah realize how awful he'd been.

Help us, dear Lord, to listen to your voice inside us—and to take notice.

Does our behaviour affect other people?
Jonah 1:11

The storm was getting worse all the time, so the sailors asked him, 'What should we do to you to stop the storm?'

There's a bear called Paddington who's so fond of marmalade sandwiches that he keeps some in reserve under his hat. Paddington was persuaded to take his money to the bank for safe keeping. He had one Very Small Coin. Later he wanted to make sure his Very Small Coin was safe, so he went to the bank. 'We haven't got *your* V.S.C. now,' said the bank manager, 'but here's one just like it.'

'You mean you haven't got *my* money?'

Paddington was shouting. People heard him. 'The bank hasn't got Paddington's money.' 'The bank has run out of money!' 'What about *our* money?' Everybody flooded into the bank, demanding their money back. What a hullabaloo!

Yes, people are affected by the way we behave. The sailors suffered because of Jonah. Let's be more thoughtful about other people.

Owning up is not enough
Jonah 1:12

Jonah answered, 'Throw me into the sea, and it will calm down. I know it is my fault that you are caught in this violent storm.'

Sometimes, if we've done something wrong, we find the courage to own up and say 'sorry', and think that's the end of it. But it's not always as easy as that. We've already decided that our behaviour affects other people, just as Paddington being stubborn and silly caused a lot of people a lot of trouble.

Saying 'sorry' is one thing. *Doing* something to put it right is another.

Jonah had owned up. He shouldn't have been on that boat in the first place. The only way for him to put things right was for him to get off it—and the only way to go was overboard.

Yet even now he wasn't willing to jump in himself—he asked the sailors to throw him in. He wouldn't say 'yes' to God with all his heart.

Trying to find a way out...
Jonah 1:13a

*Instead, the sailors tried to get the ship to shore,
rowing with all their might.*

What was it about Jonah? He'd been disobedient, unhelpful, not willing to come clean with the truth. Yet the sailors couldn't bring themselves to throw him overboard. They desperately wanted to save his life if they could. In spite of everything, Jonah had something special about him... he knew God.

The storm was getting worse, the waves were getting higher, yet these tired, kind-hearted sailors actually tried to row the boat to safety. Notice that Jonah made no attempt to help them!

Sometimes, for the very best reasons, like those sailors we try to avoid doing what God wants. Does it work?

*Dear Lord, help us not to
make excuses for not
doing what
you want.*

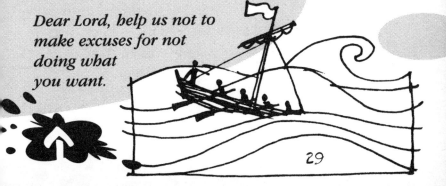

29

...and failing!
Jonah 1:13b

***But the storm was getting worse and worse,
and they got nowhere.***

Have you ever been out walking with a group of people when somebody looks at the map and says, 'Look, I know a better way.' A short cut? Beware! This usually means that you tramp through lots of fields where you shouldn't be, clamber over walls, wade through bogs and go round in circles, and everybody ends up bad-tempered.

If there's a path marked on the map, it's best to take it.

God had marked out a path for Jonah, and no amount of running away, hiding in holds or pulling on oars would alter it. Jonah would have to take God's amazing way in the end. There was no escaping the God who made the sea.

Rocks

Jonah 1:10–13
Things to do

If you were the captain...

Just remember:

1. You cannot *stop* a sailing boat.
2. You cannot go backwards.
3. You have to keep the bows of the boat heading into the wind, or it will roll over.
4. You have to keep the boat moving, or you won't be able to steer it.
5. All you can do is 'tack', that is, going a little bit to the left and a little bit to the right.

Draw a picture or a chart of a boat on the stormy sea and decide what you would do to get it safely through the storm if you were the captain.

Toby + Trish — It's an ill wind

You weren't long on your bicycle, Trish

The bad news: the wind blew me back. The good news: it's my favourite programme. Sshh!

31

Blaming God
Jonah 1:14

So they cried out to the Lord, 'O Lord, we pray, don't punish us with death for taking this man's life! You, O Lord, are responsible for all this: it is your doing.'

When something goes wrong, we immediately look round for somebody to blame: Mum, the boy next door, big sister, the cat—even God. When some terrible disaster happens in the world, we say, 'Why does God allow this?' It's sometimes difficult to understand why these things happen.

But here we know *exactly* why the storm is blowing and the ship is in trouble. It's Jonah. He tried to go west when God told him to go east!

Quite often, if we think about it, we can trace a terrible event to one person being selfish, or disobedient, or careless. Then other people suffer.

Please, Lord, make me careful not to do anything that may hurt or harm other people.

Into the sea with him!
Jonah 1:15

Then they picked Jonah up and threw him into the sea, and it calmed down at once.

Sometimes, if you've been tossing about in bed, you wake up to find you're all tangled up in your duvet. The more you thrash about and struggle, the worse it gets. Better to be still and think about it, and you'll soon be sorted out.

The sailors were thrashing about, tangled up in a situation they didn't understand and which was getting worse. But in Psalm 46 God says, 'Stop struggling—and know that I am God.'

By throwing Jonah into the sea, the sailors had stopped struggling against God. They were beginning to know God, although they didn't realize it.

Immediately, everything became peaceful. It was unbelievable. True, Jonah had disappeared under the water, but God was now able to get on with things as he had planned.

23

The effects of God's action
Jonah 1:16

This made the sailors so afraid of the Lord that they offered a sacrifice and promised to serve him.

Can you imagine how the sailors felt? First of all, Jonah turns up on their boat and there's something different about him. Now, it seems he's actually given his own life so that they may be saved. (No wonder Jesus loved this story.)

In the storm, and then in the stillness, they could see the power of Jonah's God. It was as though they'd taken part in a great drama that was being acted out on their boat. Only this was for real!

The word 'fear' can mean slightly different things. They didn't have the 'knocking-at-the-knees' kind of fear—they felt a great awe and respect for the Lord. So... even when we're foolish, God can use us to reach other people. His power can change lives, even when *we* get it wrong.

34

Gulp!
Jonah 1:17

At the Lord's command a large fish swallowed Jonah, and he was inside the fish for three days and nights.

Well! What a surprise! Just as Jonah thought his end had come, a large mouth opened up and swallowed him. I guess the fish was a bit surprised, too. The only person who wasn't surprised was God, who had planned it all.

As Jonah realized what had happened to him—I imagine being swallowed is rather an unusual feeling—he would lose track of time. There's no sunrise in the tummy of a fish. It's dark all the time, and a bit noisy, I should think. One thing's certain—Jonah had no watch!

Later on, he reported that he was in the fish for three days and three nights, so we can take it that it seemed like that—a fairly long time.

Our God is certainly a God of surprises.

GULP!

The sperm whale

We don't know exactly what happened to Jonah, but we have a pretty good idea.

There are several enormous creatures that live in the Mediterranean Sea. Jonah's 'fish' may have been a sperm whale, which has a throat wide enough to swallow a person. (It is believed to have actually happened to someone in 1927 and he lived to tell the tale!)

The sperm whale eats fish, so it has teeth. But, like all other whales, it cannot see very far as there is not much light under water.

36

A whale is a mammal that lives in the water and spends a lot of time swimming in the great depths of the ocean. But, because it is a mammal, every three-quarters of an hour or so it has to come to the surface for air. Then it holds its breath as it plunges to the depths again. (This ties in well with the story of Jonah.) Under its skin, a whale has a thick layer of blubber, or fat, to keep it warm in deep waters.

37

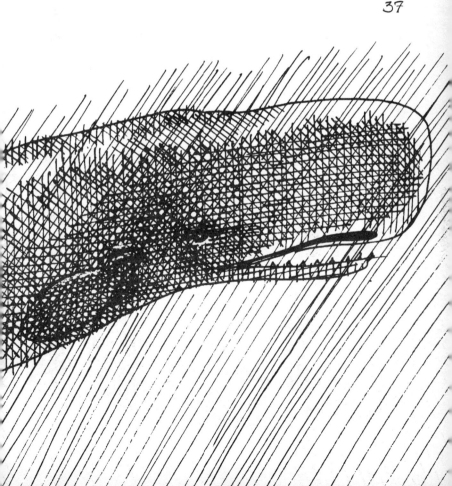

Jonah 1:14-17

Things to do

Jonah's ticket

SECOND CLASS TICKET

One person ___ Jonah ___

From ___ Joppa

To ___ Spain

Draw a ticket for the Joppa-to-Spain ferry. Soak it in water, then dry it, so that it looks like the ticket that came out of Jonah's pocket when he got back to dry land.

Toby + Trish — Just the ticket

Where did I leave my ticket for the pop concert?

Looks like somebody else is going

Deep, deep as the deepest sea
Jonah 2:1

*From deep inside the fish Jonah
prayed to the Lord his God.*

Hurray! At last! Jonah has prayed to his God. If only he could have done that before, he would have saved a whole heap of trouble both for himself and for all those sailors.

It's strange that just now, when there seems to be so much separating him from God—the sea and the whale, to say the least—Jonah finds he can finally pray.

We sometimes feel, particularly if we've been disobedient or silly, that there's something like a great wall separating us from God. We can't reach him. But, just as it says in the song that is sometimes sung in church, God's love is everywhere:

*Wide, wide as the ocean,
High as the heaven above,
Deep, deep as the deepest sea
Is my Saviour's love.*

The God who listens
Jonah 2:2

'In my distress, O Lord, I called to you, and you answered me. From deep in the world of the dead I cried for help, and you heard me.'

Have you ever made a telephone call to a friend and heard a strange voice at the other end of the line saying, 'There is nobody here at the moment to take your call, but...' You have to talk to an answering machine: nobody is listening. THIS SENDS ME HOPPING MAD! I hate talking to a machine.

What a blessing that God is not like that. Wherever you are, even like poor Jonah calling from the bottom of the sea, God hears. No matter what time it is, God is always at home.

Jonah knew this, and what a difference it made to him. He'd been feeling so bad, he thought he was going to die.

Hold on, Jonah. God has heard you, and will answer.

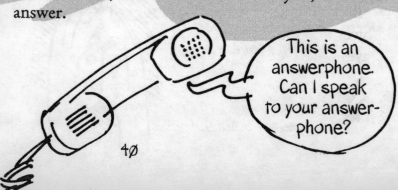

This is an answerphone. Can I speak to your answer-phone?

The bottom of the sea
Jonah 2:3

'You threw me down into the depths, to the very bottom of the sea, where the waters were all round me, and all your mighty waves rolled over me.'

We once had a dog called Sam who reminded me of Eeyore, Pooh Bear's donkey friend. They were both very GLOOMY. Sam thought everything that happened was aimed at *him*, so he was bad-tempered as well as gloomy. (Not a bit like Toby and Trish's dog, Boomerang!)

Jonah's feeling gloomy—again! Maybe with some reason—being inside a fish can't be much fun. But see how often the word 'me' appears in his complaint. Jonah, like Sam, was completely taken up with himself. He was feeling sorry for himself, instead of thinking about God's reason for all this.

But at least Jonah is starting to realize how powerful God is. He could see that the mighty waves were God's waves.

Father, help us not to be so taken up with our problems that we lose sight of your purposes.

Feeling far from God
Jonah 2:4

'I thought I had been banished from your presence and would never see your holy Temple again.'

In one of my favourite films, *Zorba the Greek*, two people are making a promise to each other. Suddenly, Zorba, who often gets things wrong, says, 'We must do this in the sight of God. Come outside, then God can see us better.' Wrong again, Zorba!

God is not limited to the open sky, or to temples and churches. No matter where we are, or what we're doing, God is close and can see us. You'd have thought Jonah would have learnt that by now. As for being banished from God's presence... never! It was Jonah who had tried to banish God.

A boy was playing football and as he scored a goal he shouted, 'Look, Lord Jesus, look!' The Lord is as close as that.

Don't look, Lord. I missed

Pictures of the deep
Jonah 2:5

'The water came over me and choked me; the sea covered me completely, and seaweed was wrapped round my head.'

Have you ever had a ride on a ghost train? In the nearly-dark, everything seems to be green or red. There are strange noises, and horrid things come at you or drop and wrap around your head. It's a nightmare world. But you know it's not real—soon you'll be back in the normal world again.

Jonah was in a nightmare world that *was* real. Strange noises; things coming at him in the nearly-dark, covering him and wrapping round him. Worst of all, Jonah didn't know whether he would ever be free again. Would he ever be back in the normal world again?

But God knew, and at the right time would bring Jonah out safely.

Lord God, keep me free from all things that can frighten or trap me.

43

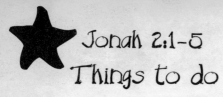

Jonah 2:1-5

Things to do

Bottom of the sea

What do fish look like at the bottom of the sea? Some are shaped so that they can flatten themselves on the sea bed. Some hide in the sand. Some have large eyes. Some are very big. Some have long feelers to help them find their way through the dark. Some look very gloomy. What kind of fish would you imagine there to be? Draw a picture of it and give it a name.

Dark places...
Jonah 2:6a

'I went down to the very roots of the mountains, into the land whose gates lock shut for ever.'

Stand in front of a mirror and grin. You see a range of pearly mountains—your teeth. But there's more to your teeth than you can see. They have roots firmly planted in your gums—which are firmly planted on your jaw.

It's the same with mountains. We gaze in wonder at them, but there's more to mountains than we can see. Their roots are firmly planted on the ocean bed.

Jonah was at the very bottom—he could go no lower. Even today, parts of the sea bed have never been explored.

Sometimes, when things are tough, we think we've hit rock-bottom. And that is the time when we can put our feet firmly on this solid, everlasting rock and give ourselves a good push upwards!

Lord, help us to know that you are our everlasting rock.

45

...don't last for ever
Jonah 2:6b

'But you, O Lord, brought me back from the depths alive.'

Sometimes, like Jonah, we moan when things aren't going our way. It's tough. But afterwards it's good to look back, just for a moment. We'll be surprised at what we've learned. It would be nice if life was always easy, but we learn lots of important things when we're up against it. Things about ourselves, about other people, and about God.

It was God who brought Daniel, unharmed, out of the lion's den, and Paul and Silas out of the deep dungeon. Both these stories are in the Bible. Even disobedient Jonah will be saved—after he's learnt a few lessons!

So what have *we* to fear? The God of Daniel, Paul, Silas and Jonah is our God. He is with us and will bring us safely out of all our difficult times.

Message received
Jonah 2:7

'When I felt my life slipping away, then, O Lord, I prayed to you, and in your holy Temple you heard me.'

Jonah, thinking his last hour has come, looks back longingly to a place of peace and light where he felt God was. But he is comforted that, even from the depths, God has heard him. A big step forward for Jonah!

After a fortnight of glorious sun, it's hard coming back from my favourite Greek holidays. We fly in sunshine above the clouds, then drop down to land, sucking boiled sweets to stop our ears from popping. Then, as we enter the clouds, the cabin goes dark, the sun disappears, and we feel it's gone for ever. What an awful feeling!

But above the clouds, the sun is still shining. It hasn't gone anywhere; it's just hidden from us.

Sometimes, we feel that God isn't there any more. But he is, full of light and love, and, what is more, HE ALWAYS HEARS US.

All that glitters is not God

Jonah 2:8

'Those who worship worthless idols have abandoned their loyalty to you.'

Just a minute, Jonah! What's all this about abandoning loyalty to God? You're a good one to talk!

Jonah has a point, though. A lot of people spend a lot of time thinking about worthless idols—things that don't last.

There's a story about an old weaver, Silas Marner, who lived and worked alone. Every night he took out his gold coins and counted them carefully. Then one day somebody stole them, and his life was turned upside down. He started mixing with his neighbours... at first hoping to find his money, then because he found he needed people. One night, in the firelight, he saw what he thought was his gold on the rug. But it was a little girl with golden curls. She soon meant more to him than his gold ever did.

Dear Lord, help us to love the people we meet more than we love the things which we have.

I'm not taking Boomerang out in the rain because I'll get wet

Jonah sees sense at last
Jonah 2:9

'But I will sing praises to you; I will offer you a sacrifice and do what I have promised. Salvation comes from the Lord!'

Let's not put out the flags just yet! Although Jonah is now ready to obey God's command and praise him, he still has some thinking to do.

There's a famous play about Thomas à Becket of Canterbury Cathedral. In it Thomas says that the worst thing is to do the right thing for the wrong reason.

Why do we go to church? Because it makes us feel good and because our best friend goes? Or is it simply that we love the Lord Jesus? Why are we friendly with that boy at school? Because he lives in a big house and lets us use his computer? Or do we really like him?

It seems that Jonah is still looking down his nose at Nineveh. He will go out of a sense of duty—not out of love. But at least he will go!

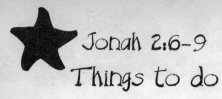

Jonah 2:6-9
Things to do

One-to-one

Make a telephone that works! You need two empty plastic washing-up liquid bottles. Cut off the bottom six centimetres—this is the bit you need. Ask a grown-up to help you make a *tiny* hole in the middle of the bottom of each piece, using the point of a compass from your maths set. Thread a long length of thin parcel string through each hole and knot securely on the inside.

Give one end to a friend and ask them to go into the next room. Make sure the string is pulled taut and that nothing is touching it along its length. As you can only speak or listen at one time, you need to say 'over' when you have finished speaking.

It's fish fingers for tea

Toby + Trish Over and out

Go into the next room and think of something and I'll see if I can pick it up in here

Now for a bit of peace

50

Back on dry land
Jonah 2:10

Then the Lord ordered the fish to spew Jonah up on the beach, and it did.

We begin to see why Jesus thought so much of Jonah, in spite of his faults. Jesus himself, after far more suffering than Jonah experienced, was also to spend three days in the 'depths'—in a stone tomb.

So... after three days and nights, Jonah shot out on to the beach. Just imagine the joy of fresh air, the refreshing shallows of the Mediterranean Sea, the sun shining. Daylight. Being in that fish must have been worse than living in a dustbin.

After Jonah had recovered a bit, I'm sure he would splash in the sparkling waves to get rid of the smell of the fish!

Jesus is the light of the world, and he wants to bring us out into the daylight and the sparkle of his love and friendship.

One more time
Jonah 3:1

Once again the Lord spoke to Jonah.

When you're learning to ride a bicycle and you fall off, the only thing to do is to get right back on again. Otherwise you might never ride a bicycle.

So it was with Jonah. He had 'fallen off' badly. But God gave him a second chance.

God is so loving and patient with us that he often gives us a second chance. Maybe we've missed an opportunity to make a friend, help somebody, or put something right. Let's make sure that, if God does 'wind back the tape' for us today, we grab that second chance. It may not come again.

Go for it, Jonah!

Get the message?
Jonah 3:2

The Lord said, 'Go to Nineveh, that great city, and proclaim to the people the message I have given you.'

Have you ever played a party game called 'Chinese Whispers'? You all sit round in a circle and somebody thinks of a very short message. Then they whisper it, very quietly, to the next person—just once! That person whispers it to the next, and so on. The last person then tells everybody what the message is that has come to them. You'd be surprised how the message changes as it's passed along the line!

Notice how God says to Jonah, '…the message I have given you'. Not any old message. God's message. From the beginning of the Bible until this very day, God has been telling his people what he wants them to say to others.

If we take time to talk to Jesus and listen carefully to what he wants to say to us—through the Bible, through others and through our own thoughts—he will give us things to say for him.

Dear Lord, use my mouth to speak to others.

Nineveh at last
Jonah 3:3

So Jonah obeyed the Lord and went to Nineveh, a city so large that it took three days to walk through it.

Hurray! It's a miracle! God's man is now in the right place! If there was a newspaper in heaven—*The Heavenly Times*—this would have made the headlines.

But let's think for a moment about what's really going on. If we'd followed Jonah into Nineveh we'd have lost him in the crowds in the first minute. He was just one little man amongst the thousands of people who lived in this important city, which was roughly as big as London.

To make matters worse, these people had no time for God—they were too busy doing things their way. (Dare we say it—Jonah must have felt a bit like a fish out of water!)

But all this would change—simply because Jonah finally obeyed the Lord.

Let's get going
Jonah 3:4a

*Jonah started through the city,
and after walking a whole day...*

Jonah, God's messenger, was not happy. As he walked through the hot streets, he looked at the people there and he really disliked them. But he had to get to the city centre so that his message could be heard by the important people who lived there—even the king himself.

What a shame that Jonah didn't look at the people with love as he walked. I used to know a monk who walked through a city every day, smiling and waving at everybody and saying, 'Good morning'. He wore sandals and a shabby brown habit whatever the weather. But his smile was like sunshine —it made you feel warm and cheerful. What a good advertisement for God!

*Dear Lord, help me to be
a good advertisement for you.*

55

Nineveh

Jonah 2:10 — 3:4
Things to do

City quiz

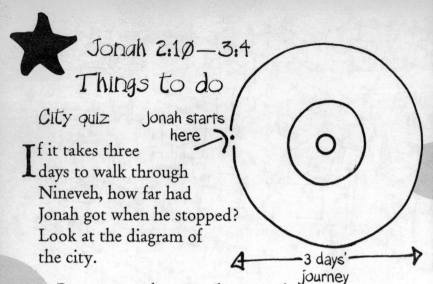

Jonah starts here

If it takes three days to walk through Nineveh, how far had Jonah got when he stopped? Look at the diagram of the city.

3 days' journey

1. Put a cross where Jonah stopped.
2. How far from the centre was he when he stopped?

Nineveh was so large that there were probably three or four towns on the outskirts which had become part of the city. Take a modern map and look for the biggest city. Can you see any towns on the outskirts which have become part of the city? Using the scale of the map as a guide, see if you can work out how many miles across the city is. How long would it take to walk to the middle?

Toby + Trish — Nature quiz

Question: Which is the fastest bird in level flight?

Something like a kestrel?

Not quite! Answer: A duck!

58

What! Only six weeks?
Jonah 3:4b

...he proclaimed, 'In forty days Nineveh will be destroyed!'

Have you ever noticed that when you're waiting for something nice to happen—Christmas or your birthday—time seems to crawl by? It will *never* come. But if you know something that you're not looking forward to is going to happen—an exam or a visit to the dentist—it's on you before you can say 'snip-snap'. (Just ask Mary Poppins!)

'Six weeks,' said Jonah (and probably thought, 'serves them right'). To the people of Nineveh it must have meant 'no time left'.

It's a mark of God's love that, although he is Lord of everything in the world, he has given us freedom to choose right or wrong. But having chosen, we must be prepared to take the consequences of our actions.

Only 40 shopping days to Christmas

Dear God, when we have a choice, help us to make the right one.

Stop what you're doing, folks...
Jonah 3:5a

The people of Nineveh believed God's message.

I have a friend who went on a caravanning holiday to France. Unfortunately, as he drove his large caravan off the ferry, he forgot something vitally important: in France you drive on the *right-hand* side of the road. He drove straight off the ferry and on to a huge roundabout—going the wrong way round. Five lanes of traffic coming into the roundabout went mad! There was chaos. Then a little French policeman bravely stepped into the middle of it all, blew his whistle, and sorted it out.

Nineveh was a city in chaos. Jonah had no whistle. But he did have God. He stood in the middle of a city he didn't like and delivered God's message. And the people stopped to listen.

...whoever you are...
Jonah 3:5b

So they decided that everyone should fast, and all the people, from the greatest to the least...

Jonah and his message had caused a sensation. Everybody was talking about it. Imagine the news headlines (if there had been television in those days—which there wasn't):

'Our main story tonight is the forecast of doom by a Galilean prophet. We go straight over to Nineveh to our on-the-spot reporter.

'Yes, here we are in the centre of this great city and, as you can see, this square and all the streets around are packed with people—both rich and poor. And they're all talking about Jonah and his message from God. All the cafés and restaurants are closed because everybody is fasting. Yes... everybody. I'm hoping to get Jonah to the microphone...

'No, he doesn't want to speak. He seems stunned by what is happening. He must be a very happy man to see how well his message from God has been received. Back to the studio.'

Was Jonah happy? We shall see.

43

...and show you're sorry
Jonah 3:5c

...put on sackcloth to show that they had repented.

There was no mistaking the shame of the Nineveh folks.

In the past when people were sad or ashamed of themselves, they showed their feelings by emptying ashes on their heads, wearing itchy old sacking and walking barefoot.

Nowadays, apart from wearing something black for funerals, in western countries at least we find it hard to show our grief—or that we're sorry for something we've done—which is sometimes a pity.

In some churches, however, a small amount of ash is smeared on people's foreheads on Ash Wednesday—the day after Pancake Day—and kept there for as long as possible until Easter Day.

For us to know the forgiveness of God, because Jesus died for us on the cross, we must first feel sorry.

Help us, Lord, to feel sorry when we've done wrong. Then happy that you have forgiven us.

Jonah 3:4-5
Things to do
Sandwich-board

A sandwich-board isn't a table with a snack on it—it's a board that people sometimes carry about to advertise something: a new shop that's opening in the town; a new show at the theatre; or even what God says in the Bible. You might have seen somebody carrying one in your local town.

Imagine Jonah carrying a board telling the crowds in Nineveh about God's message. Make a board, like the one in the picture, out of a cereal box and, on one side, write what Jonah's board would say. On the other side, write what you would want to tell people about God's love. You could use a Bible verse—John 3:16 would be a good one. Ask a grown-up to help you find it in John's Gospel.

You might like to make a full-sized board that can be worn, and take it to church.

Toby + Trish — Wanted

The King of kings
Jonah 3:6

When the king of Nineveh heard about it, he got up from his throne, took off his robe, put on sackcloth, and sat down in ashes.

Everything the king does here is so definite, so deliberate, that there can be no mistaking the shame that he feels.

When Jesus' mother, Mary, first found that she was going to have a baby she sang a hymn of praise to God. You can find it in Luke's Gospel.

'He has brought down mighty kings from their thrones,' she sang. Perhaps she was remembering how God had worked with Jonah, the prophet from Galilee where she herself lived, to deliver his message.

God is the King of kings, and his kingdom will last for ever. People kneel down in front of kings to show their respect, which is why many people kneel down to pray.

 *Dear God, King of kings, thank you for ruling your kingdom with love.*

An order from the king
Jonah 3:7

The king sent out a proclamation to the people of Nineveh: 'This is an order from the king and his officials: no one is to eat anything; all persons, cattle, and sheep are forbidden to eat or drink.'

Just imagine what would happen if we were all ordered to stop eating. (What food would you miss most?) Imagine if all the supermarkets, bakers, greengrocers, butchers and fishmongers were closed and none of the takeaway restaurants had anything to take away. Nothing.

The king gave the order because he wanted the people to think about how sorry they were for doing wrong, rather than about what they were going to fill their tummies with. What a reminder to the people their hungry tummies would have been! What a mooing, baaing, woofing and miaowing there must have been from the hungry animals!

We don't often give up food nowadays to show that we are sorry. But this is, of course, the reason behind why we sometimes give up sweets in Lent. Maybe we should remember to be more thoughtful about our food every day. God has given it to us to enjoy, but not to be greedy or wasteful with.

My favourite colour is tomato ketchup

When the colour goes out of life
Jonah 3:8a

'All persons and animals must wear sackcloth.'

Colours are important to how we feel: red for warmth, yellow for sunshine. Think of some more.

Nineveh had become sad-coloured. Everybody wore sackcloth—grey, shapeless and itchy. Compared to them, Jonah, in spite of his adventures, must have looked quite smart. Even the animals outdid him in drabness.

This is what happens in the end when people choose their own ways instead of God's. Their lives become drab, without true excitement, without colour.

The flag that flies from a ship's mast is called its 'colours'. It shows which country the ship belongs to. We talk about 'nailing our colours to the mast' when we want to show what we believe in. Have you 'nailed your colours to the mast' for Jesus?

Dear Lord, help me to know the colour and true excitement of living my life for you.

Do we really mean it?
Jonah 3:8b

'Everyone must pray earnestly to God and must give up his wicked behaviour and his evil actions.'

The important word in today's Bible verse is 'earnestly', meaning sincerely, from the heart. The people of Nineveh were ordered by the king to take a good look at their evil ways and then pray for forgiveness. There might have been a few who prayed in order to save their skins (doing the right thing for the wrong reason). But most were truly sorry.

With all that sackcloth and ashes about, the people looked sorry on the *outside*. But that is not enough. They were now ordered to feel sorry from the *inside*, where it really counts.

It's easy for us to say 'sorry' when we've done something wrong—'I'll never do it again.' But do we really mean it in our hearts, where it counts?

They shouldn't say 'walkies' if they don't mean it

Dear Lord, let my mouth say what my heart feels.

67

The God who sees
Jonah 3:10a

God saw what they did.

When our family goes on holiday to a Greek island, we love to travel on old Greek buses. It's great fun! We sway about over mountain passes and clatter through olive groves, packed like sardines in a can. (The bus always carries three times as many people as it should.)

Often, just above the windscreen inside, there's something a bit unusual that always makes us think.

In the cool Greek evening we catch another bus. This bus is almost empty and we travel at a fantastic speed with the driver singing and the windows rattling. And this unusual object is there on this bus, too. It's an 'eye' looking down the bus. Sometimes it's a picture; sometimes it's made of glass. It's looking down at each one of us just as it did in the morning bustle.

The 'eye' is there to remind us that God sees everything we are doing.

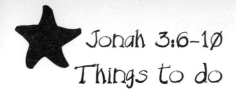

Jonah 3:6-10

Things to do

Sorry!

'Sorry' can be the hardest word to say. Next time you have to say it, why not make a flag. Ask a grown-up to help you cut the flag shape out of a scrap of material or card. Then cut the letters to make the word SORRY out of coloured scraps of material and stick them to the card or cloth flag. Stick one edge of the flag to a small stick, or piece of dowelling, and wave it round the door.

It might just make the person you are saying 'sorry' to laugh, instead of being cross with you!

Toby + Trish — Never again

I'm never going to say sorry again

You said that yesterday

Sorry!

69

Actions speak louder than words
Jonah 3:10b

God saw that they had given up their wicked behaviour.

Toad in *Wind in the Willows* was always sticking out his chest and saying what a clever toad he was and how he was such a superb driver of motor cars. This is funny because he really wasn't good at anything, and when he drove a motor car it always crashed!

There's worse! When Toad was told by Badger to pull himself together he wept loudly and said how sorry he was. But the moment the door was left open he was off, up to his old tricks, driving motor cars again. He got his come-uppance in the end.

Unlike Toad, the people of Nineveh not only said they were sorry, they changed their ways to prove it.

So... to sum up. Being sorry comes in three stages:

FEELING...

SAYING...

CHANGING...

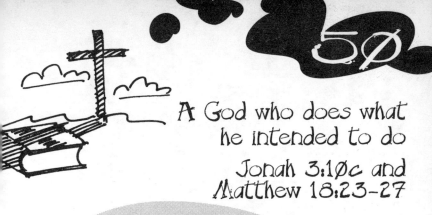

A God who does what he intended to do
Jonah 3:10c and Matthew 18:23-27

So God changed his mind and did not punish them as he had said he would.
(Verse 10c)

If God heaves sighs of relief, he must have heaved one when the people of Nineveh said they were truly sorry. Now he could do what he'd intended to do all along—forgive them.

Our God is very loving. But he won't pretend that wickedness isn't there when it's as plain as the nose on your face. Loving means seeing people as they really are... and still loving them. God would always far rather forgive us than punish us.

Right at the beginning of this book we asked the question, 'Why Jonah?' Answer: because he was who he was, and no one could have given God's message to the people of Nineveh quite like he did.

A long time after Jonah, God proved even more how much he wants to forgive us. He sent his Son, Jesus, to take the blame for all the wrong things we have done. Jesus did this on the cross.

What a

relief!

Someone's not happy
Jonah 4:1

Jonah was very unhappy about this and became angry.

A long time ago there used to be a 'Children's Hour' on the radio. My favourite part of it was 'Toy Town', with Larry the Lamb, Ernest the policeman and a very bad-tempered character called Mr Growser. Every week he arrived on the scene shouting, 'This is disgraceful; it ought not to be allowed!' and called for Ernest the policeman. Mr Growser was just like Jonah.

Jonah has a big problem. Although he loves and worships God, he can't understand why God doesn't think exactly as *he* does. He's trying to bring God down to size—*his* size—and he's angry because God does what *God* wants.

'This is disgraceful; it ought not to be allowed!' What do you think?

So *that's* why he did it!
Jonah 4:2a

So Jonah prayed, 'Lord, didn't I say before I left home that this is just what you would do? That's why I did my best to run away to Spain!'

So! At last! The truth is out about Jonah. He finally tells God what God knew all along—but it was good for Jonah to put it into words and admit it. He hadn't run away from God because he was a coward. He'd run away because he *knew* that God would forgive the people of Nineveh if they said they were sorry and changed their ways. Jonah couldn't bear the fact that Nineveh was going to be let off.

But look at the pain, the hurt and bitterness in his heart. He'd been a trouble to himself as well as to other people.

It can happen that we sometimes dislike somebody so much that we can't bear anybody else to like them, let alone love them.

If this does happen, remember what Jonah says next as he looks at God…

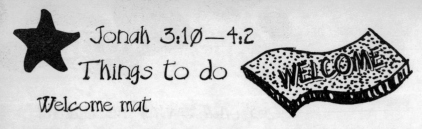

Jonah 3:10 — 4:2
Things to do

Welcome mat

The trouble with belonging to a church is that new people are always discovering God's love and joining, and some people find that uncomfortable.

How would you react if somebody joined your football or netball team, or your particular group of friends, and was so good at scoring goals or thinking up good ideas for your friends to do that they made you feel useless? You might feel put out. You might even start not to like them very much. You might even feel just a bit cross.

Make yourself a welcome mat out of a piece of card.

Put the word WELCOME on it, big and bold, and decorate the letters. Then display the mat somewhere where you'll see it every day as a reminder not to be a Mr or Miss Growser.

A God who is loving...
Jonah 4:2b

'I knew that you are a loving and merciful God...'

We've looked at Jonah. Now we'll look at God. Let's call it THE GOD FILE.

What is love? We all need to receive it, and we all need to give it. Some people have made great sacrifices because they loved.

Just before the Northern Ireland peace talks, a message came that a bomb was about to go off in a crowded police station there. A policeman, Michael Willets, managed to get everybody out, but there wasn't even time to close the door as the bomb exploded. So he deliberately stood in the doorway —he became the door—to protect others from the blast. Michael was killed, but he saved the lives of those who hadn't managed to get clear. He made a great sacrifice because of his love for others. He was awarded the George Cross medal for his bravery. That's love.

When Jesus died on that awful cross for you and me, he made a great sacrifice. It was God's love given in all its fulness.

The God file (2)
Jonah 4:2c

'...*always patient*...'

Two sorts of people fish from the harbour at Bridlington. There are the children, who can't wait to catch a fish. They throw in their lines, pull them out, check the bait, throw them in again, wiggle them about, then pull them out again to see if they've caught anything yet. Usually they haven't.

Then there are the old fishermen. They sit like statues. Waiting. Now and then the line wrapped around their first finger twitches slightly. That is when they *know* they've caught a fish.

Being patient is difficult. Look at the shops: 'Buy now—pay next year.' Faster computer software. Instant coffee. Fast food. Let's stop for a breath!

We need to look at God, who will wait for as long as it takes. That's patience.

Dear Lord, help me to be patient, and thank you for being patient with me.

The God file (3)
Jonah 4:2d

'...always kind.'

Once, on holiday on a Greek island called Samos, our family visited the Valley of the Nightingales. We walked in cool shade, surrounded by sweet singing. And then we went on walking, up a bare mountainside in the blazing sunshine to a tiny village called Manolates. We arrived feeling hot, thirsty and tired.

Nobody was about. Then an old man came out of a poor little square house. He was carrying a plate of juicy cherries. They were still wet from his careful washing. The man was blind, but he'd heard us coming, realized that we would be hot and tired, and brought us what he had.

Putting yourself in somebody else's shoes, realizing what they need, and giving it to them (it may be cherries, or time, or a listening ear)—that's kindness.

God knows what we need, and he will give it to us.

Jonah takes his bat home
Jonah 4:3

'Now, Lord, let me die. I am better off dead than alive.'

Sometimes when you're playing cricket or rounders with your friends, the person who owns the bat thinks they should win. They don't like being bowled out and, when they are, they don't want to play any more. They 'take their bat home'.

Jonah was taking his bat home. He didn't want to play any more. It wasn't as if his mission had failed. It had been a tremendous success—from God's point of view.

That was the trouble. It hadn't been a success from Jonah's point of view. He was still stubborn. He refused to see the people of Nineveh as God saw them. So… he was taking his bat home.

'Dear Lord, help me not to be stubborn, but to see things from your point of view.

Hiding behind our faces
Jonah 4:4

The Lord answered,
'What right have you to be angry?'

When you go to a friend's party, you sometimes end up having your face painted. Somebody arrives carrying a big box of fascinating things—sticks of coloured make-up; glitter; false hair and special stickers. Before you know it, you've been transformed into somebody (or something) else. A little boy I know became Spiderman, complete with webs and glitter. At least, his face did. Behind it he was just the same.

People know us, and how we are, from our faces. From our eyes; our mouths; our expressions. But Jonah was hiding behind his face. Hiding from God. Therefore all his anger and resentment was locked up inside his head. Even when God spoke to him he wouldn't answer.

Jonah had no reason to be angry—but try telling him that.

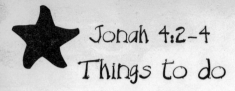

Jonah 4:2-4

Things to do

Pluses and minuses

A battery has a '+' at the top and a '-' at the bottom. Ask a grown-up to show you.

Take a piece of card 20 cm square. Draw a line from top to bottom, 2 cm in from one side. Draw a second line from top to bottom, 9 cm in from the other side. Draw a large plus sign at the top of the right-hand 9 cm column and write the word 'God' underneath it. Now list all the things that you notice about God in the story of Jonah in this column. Draw a large minus sign at the top of the middle 9 cm column and write the word 'Jonah' underneath it. Now list all the things that you notice about Jonah in the story.

Run some glue down the left-hand 2 cm strip and glue the card to form a cylinder. Cut out two circles of card to fit over the ends of the cylinder.

Put your battery by your bedside table as a reminder to put some pluses in everything you do!

Toby + Trish — Powerless

My Walkman needs new batteries

My batteries need a new Walkman

82

Jonah sulks
Jonah 4:5

Jonah went out east of the city and sat down. He made a shelter for himself and sat in its shade, waiting to see what would happen to Nineveh.

There is a lovely true story about a little dog called Bobby who lived at Greyfriars in Edinburgh. When his master died, Bobby wouldn't leave his side. Even after his master was buried, the little dog huddled by his grave waiting for him to come so they could be together again. Of course, it never happened and, after a long time, Bobby died and was buried close by.

You can almost feel sorry for poor old Jonah. There he huddled, all by himself, in his little shelter, waiting for something to happen that never would.

He'd become so obsessed with his dislike of the people of Nineveh that he obviously couldn't think straight any more.

Although God had changed thousands of hearts in Nineveh, his prophet Jonah was a much bigger problem.

Dear Lord, help my mind to be always clear and open to what you want.

The vine

Just imagine you're watching a plant actually growing! It sounds a bit like 'Jack and the Beanstalk' or speeded-up photography on a television nature programme, but in hot dry countries, when it eventually rains, vines can grow overnight. They twine their tendrils round a tree; the wall of a house; anything standing upright—even Jonah's shelter. Vines of this sort usually only live for a very short time.

85

A God who is loving, patient and kind

Jonah 4:6

Then the Lord God made a plant grow up over Jonah to give him some shade, so that he would be more comfortable. Jonah was extremely pleased with the plant.

Maybe life's not so bad after all, Jonah might have thought, sitting under the coolness of the big plant.

Trees are very important in hot Mediterranean countries. Most houses have their own tree or vine. People even try to park their cars and motorbikes under shade. Dogs and cats thankfully sprawl out in it and restaurants are often built under trees so that people can eat outside in the shade.

God… who loves us enough to send his only Son to die for us… is patient for as long as it takes… and knows exactly what we need and will provide it… He knew that Jonah needed shade.

God also knew that *words* were not enough for Jonah. So he'd prepared a lesson that would *show* Jonah his foolishness.

The lesson begins
Jonah 4:7

But at dawn the next day, at God's command, a worm attacked the plant, and it died.

There's a funny book called *Three Men in a Boat*. Harris, one of the characters, is a great show-off. He goes into Hampton Court maze in London and boasts to everybody wandering about lost: 'I'm just going into the middle, then straight out again.' A crowd of people follow him. Then it becomes obvious that Harris is as lost as everybody else (only he won't admit it).

The people of Nineveh had admitted that they'd lost their way. Jonah wouldn't.

Now the destruction was happening over *his* head. As he stared across at Nineveh the shady vine withered, its leaves dropped off, and it died.

The people of Nineveh were doing fine. It was Jonah who was having a hard time.

Loving Father, help me to know my own faults before I look at other people's.

87

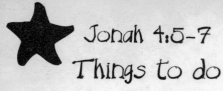

Jonah 4:5-7
Things to do

Sitting in the shade

When the sun is hot it is very uncomfortable to sit in it for very long. You need to sit in the shade. If you are on a beach, you will need an umbrella to sit under.

Using some pipe-cleaners or drinking-straws for the stems, paper for the leaves and playdough for the base, make a model of the vine that Jonah sat underneath. Cut out the leaf shapes and colour them green. Stick them to the stems with sellotape. Push the vine into the playdough base. Make a model of Jonah out of playdough or pipe-cleaners and sit him under the vine. Put your model under a bright light and move the vine to one side so that Jonah is sitting in the sun. Imagine how cross he will be when he starts to get too hot!

Toby + Trish Bright idea

Why are you wearing sun-glasses, Trish?

It's wildlife in Africa

88

I shall just get my toes tanned on holiday

Hot-headed Jonah
Jonah 4:8

After the sun had risen, God sent a hot east wind, and Jonah was about to faint from the heat of the sun beating down on his head. So he wished he were dead. 'I'm better off dead than alive,' he said.

Winnie the Pooh was… well, plump, and when he called to see his friend, Rabbit, he had difficulty squeezing through Rabbit's small door.

Once inside, Pooh ate every bit of Rabbit's delicious honey. Then, when it was time to go, he got stuck in the door. He couldn't move. There he stayed for several days until he slimmed down. Rabbit hung his washing on Pooh's back legs and, when the animals finally pulled him out, Pooh really suffered. But it was his own fault!

Here's Jonah, feeling sorry for himself—again. And it's his own fault. His troubles were his own doing. He could have been happy, together with the people of Nineveh. He could have enjoyed following his loving Lord. Jonah was his own worst enemy.

Loving Lord, help me to see that my problems can sometimes be my own fault.

Cool-headed God!

Jonah 4:9

But God said to Jonah, 'What right have you to be angry about the plant?' Jonah replied, 'I have every right to be angry—angry enough to die!'

> The geranium was OK until I sang to it!

When somebody's good at looking after plants we say they've got 'green fingers'. My daughter has green fingers. She takes tiny cuttings from plants, sticks them in a pot and in no time they're huge and flowering. She waters her plants, feeds them, re-pots them and prunes them. (I think she even sings to them when nobody's about!) And when one of them dies, as all plants must eventually, she's sorry. But not angry.

Jonah's really worked himself into a state. Obviously, he's grown fond of his plant—just him and it together through its short life. But why angry?

Jonah's all caught up with <u>himself</u>. Because the plant died, *he* was feeling uncomfortable. It was ME, ME, ME.

God knew this, but kept cool. His lesson was more important than that.

Jonah learns his lesson
Jonah 4:1Ø-11

The Lord said to Jonah, 'This plant grew up in one night and disappeared the next; you didn't do anything for it, and you didn't make it grow—yet you feel sorry for it! How much more, then, should I have pity on Nineveh, that great city. After all, it has more than 120,000 innocent children in it, as well as the animals!'

God is saying to Jonah, 'Your plant fell to the ground—but *I* made it happen so that you would see sense.' What a lot of trouble God has gone to for Jonah.

How could Jonah feel sorry when a plant dies, yet want the destruction of all the people and animals in Nineveh? Jonah's sorrow over the plant was as nothing compared to God's sorrow over even the possibility of that.

Hundreds of years later, Jesus spoke about God's love and care in much the same way. He said, 'Not even a sparrow falls to the ground without your father's consent.' And he went on to say, 'As for you, even the hairs of your head have all been counted.' (You'll find this in Matthew 10:29–30.)

We matter so much to God... you; me; the people of Nineveh; everybody; even Jonah.

91

See you in the Amazing Book of Acts!

Matthew 12:41
(The Message)
Thanks, Jonah—and goodbye

When Jonah preached to the Ninevites they changed their lives. A far greater preacher than Jonah is here...

It must have felt to Jonah like coming out of the depths again. At last he was learning of God's great love. He could also see God's wisdom, patience and care.

When you've finished reading a good book, you feel you know the people in it. It's sad to say 'goodbye'. The book of Jonah is not just a good book—it's an Amazing Book!

You can't help loving Jonah. His troubles (as ours often are) were because he refused to say to God, 'Your will be done.'

Jesus said that the people of Galilee—and he means us as well—should turn away from doing wrong things just as the people of Nineveh did. 'Because,' he said, 'there is something here greater than Jonah.' There is. It's Jesus himself. If the people of Nineveh turned to God when they heard Jonah's message, how much more should we do so when we hear *Jesus* telling us about God's love.

Thanks, Jonah, for a great adventure!

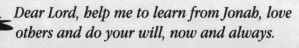

Dear Lord, help me to learn from Jonah, love others and do your will, now and always.

⭐ Jonah 4:8–11
Things to do special

How to make a 3-D model of a whale's mouth

Here's a model of Jonah inside the whale for you to make. You could tuck it inside your book and amaze your friends with the story of how God used the whale to rescue Jonah.

You'll need a sheet of stiff card 26 cm x 20 cm and two sheets of A4 paper.

1. Trace the model pieces on to the paper and cut out on the thick lines.

2. On all three pieces, fold the paper backwards along the short dotted lines and forwards along the long dotted lines.

3. Take pieces 'A' and 'B'. Glue the tabs on 'B' to the back of piece 'A', one on each side, at the bottom of the whale's mouth. (The fishes' tails should be pointing downwards.)

4. Take piece 'C'. Fold 'Jonah' backwards, so that he lies behind the centre fold of the piece. Now turn the paper over, so that Jonah is facing you. Glue the tabs to the back of piece 'A', one on each side, at the top of the whale's mouth.

5. Fold the model flat. Pieces 'B' and 'C' should fold in on themselves, behind the whale's face.

6. Take the stiff card and fold it in half.

7. Glue the tabs on piece 'A' down inside the folded card, 5.5 cm from each side edge. Open the card and see Jonah inside the whale's mouth!

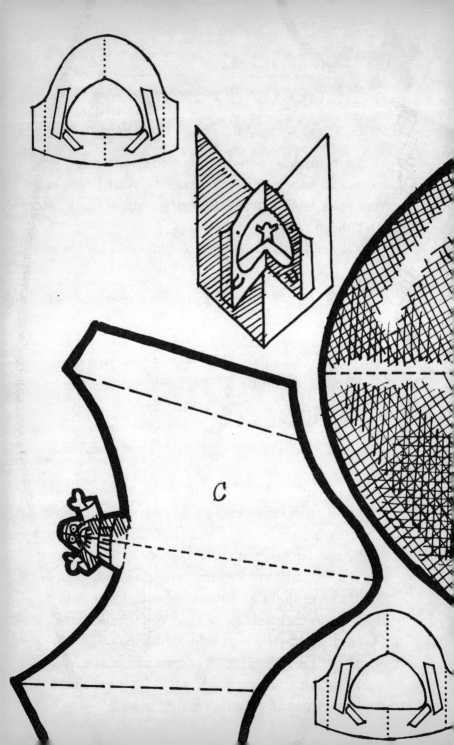

C

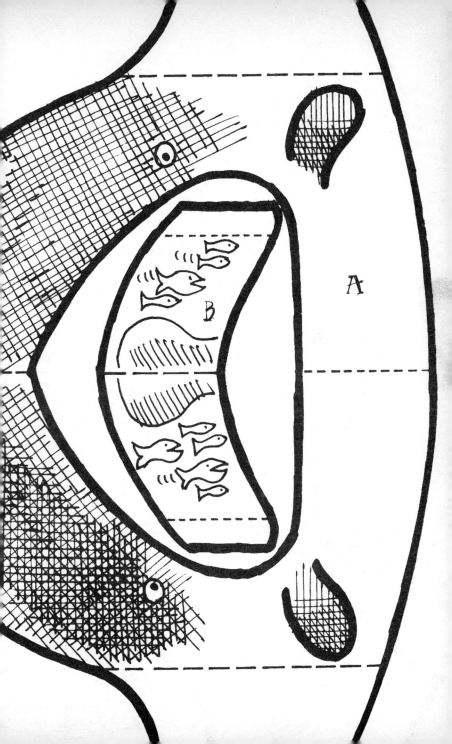